PROFESSIONAL COMMUNITY INTERVENTION TRAINING INSTITUTE

FRAMING THE THINKING PROCESS

MANUAL 2

By
Aquil Basheer

All rights reserved.

ISBN: 979-8856222639

© 2023 Aquil Basheer

No part of this book may be reproduced in any form or by any electronic or mechanical means, including information storage and retrieval systems, without permission in writing from the author.

The BUILD Program
1409 West Vernon Avenue
Los Angeles, CA 90062
info@pciti.net
https://buildprogram.org

Also by this author:

Community -Based Public Safety Violence Interdiction Training Series:

Skill Set Development: Manual 1

Peace in the Hood: Working with Gang Members to End the Violence
Peace in the Hood: Workbook

Manual 2: Framing the Thinking Process continues to put in place the building blocks of community violence intervention introduced in *Manual 1: Skill Set Development.* Manual 2 expands the introductory concepts, but more importantly starts to assist the interventionist in crafting the mental process necessary during an engagement of violence intervention. The lessons and exercises are aimed at moving the interventionist from understanding and adopting the skill set to the practical application of these rules and tools. Manual 2 also starts to draft the continuum of intervention components so they link together to achieve a safe and smooth process.

SECTION I

SCENE ANALYSIS AND PREPARATION

*Sometimes you've got to turn off your eyesight
and start using your insight.*

STRUCTURING AN ENGAGEMENT

When approaching an engagement, go over these key factors both with team mates and yourself:

GOALS: What are you trying to accomplish?

TACTICS: How will you accomplish your goals?

GUIDANCE: What is your team leadership structure?

SCHEDULE: How long will it take to accomplish your goals?

EVALUATE: How will you know you have been successful?

What are your goals? What targets are you trying to hit?	Answers	1. 2. 3.	**GOALS**
What is your methodology? What strategy will you implore?	Answers	1. 2. 3.	**TACTICS**
Who are your drivers? What does your leadership look like?	Answers	1. 2. 3.	**GUIDANCE**
What is your timetable? What are your measures of accountability?	Answers	1. 2. 3.	**SCHEDULE**
How will you test your actions? When will you know you have arrived?	Answers	1. 2. 3.	**EVALUATE**

THE RATIONALE BEHIND VIOLENCE

Violence has become a **socially acceptable** means to resolve conflicts, display power and to get needs and wants met.

Firearms are the most effective means of wielding violence. Guns produce immediate and powerful results by evoking fear and exacting harm.

Because of those results, violence can be used as a way of **increasing one's self-esteem** and **sense of self-worth**, particularly in marginalized communities where opportunities are limited.

T**he devaluation of human life** has replaced the fear of taking a life across socioeconomic boundaries.

Individual gratification of needs has become first and foremost in our society.

RATIONEL OF WHY
(Changed Mentality)

- The Use of Violence as a means to deal with multiple types of conflict and disagreements has become **SOCIALLY ACCEPTABLE!**
- Violence and Aggression is no longer a **LAST OPTION** but a **FIRST CHOICE** by so many inn everyday encounters.
- The GUN is the most effective way to impart that violence and receive instantaneous satisfaction for using that violence!
- The **DE-VALUING OF LIFE** is a common norm, in many marginalized communities, it's a badge of honor and because of the lack of options, its the first order of choice. Ironically, this is no longer isolated in structurally imbalanced communities, this mindset is becoming the **ORDER OF THE DAY NATION WIDE**. (Mass shooting-active shooter engagement)
- The **FEAR** of taking a life has been supplanted below individual gratification and personal desire.

WAYS OF COMMUNICATION

- **ETHOS:** Appeal to credibility
- **PATHOS:** Appeal to emotions
- **LOGOS:** Appeal to logic

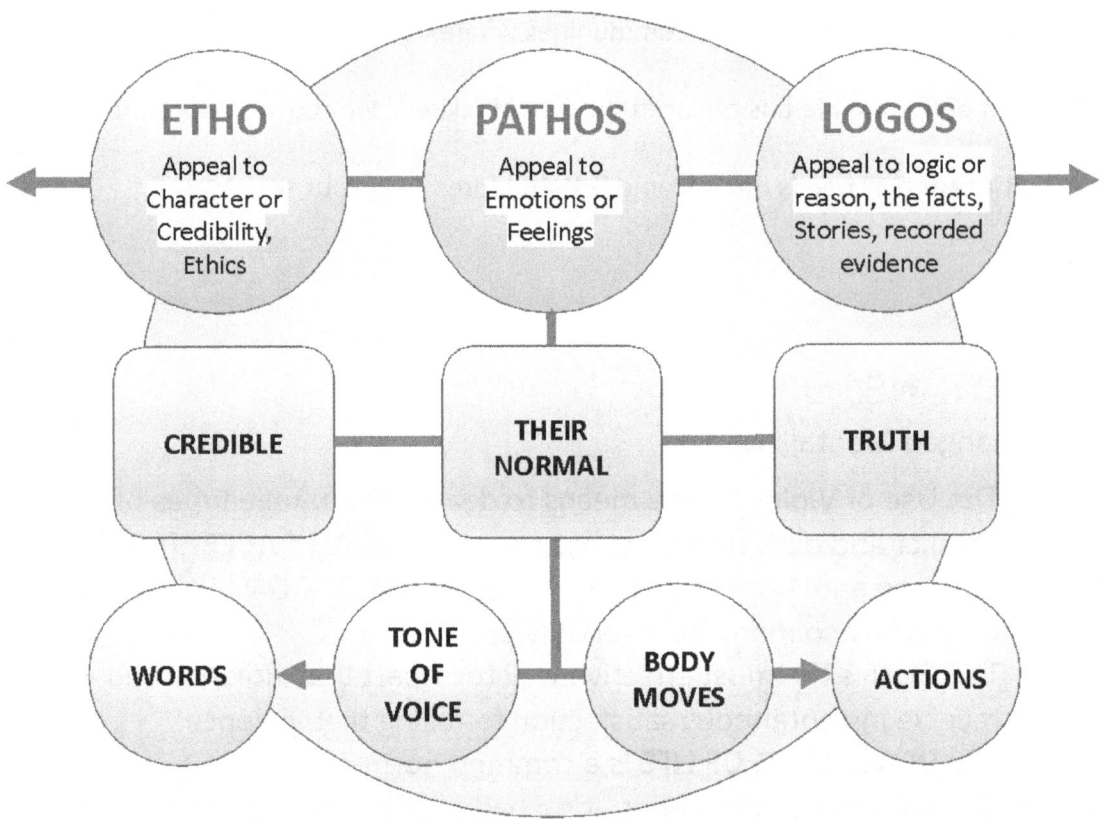

Words = Tone of voice

Body movements = Actions

STRESS LEADS TO VIOLENCE

An act of violence is often an emotional response to a stressor or trigger of some kind. Effective intervention involves pinpointing the trigger and relieving it.

- What is the stressor leading to the incident at hand?
- What level of stress is it on a scale of 1 to 10?
- What is needed to lessen or eradicate the stress?
- What is your objective? Establish a reasonable expectation.
- Decide on a course of action to accomplish that objective. What resources can you bring?

ANALYZING A VIOLENT OR THREATENING SITUATION

Use the **ARRIVE** formula to make a quick analysis:

*A*_____

*R*_____

*R*_____

*I*_____

*V*_____

*E*_____

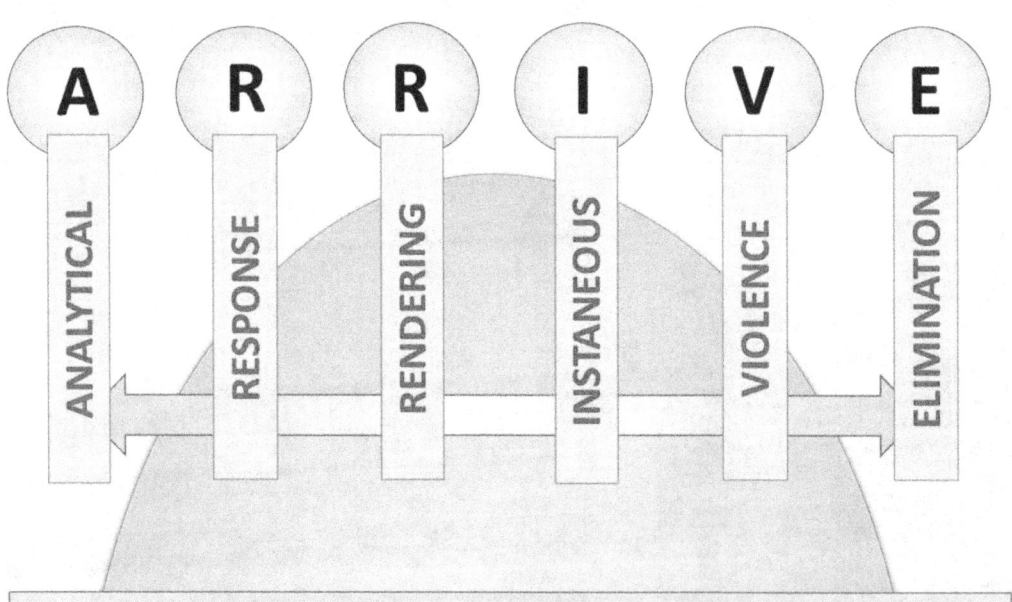

SECTION II

ENGAGEMENT & EXECUTION

Don't act on impulse.

Strategize and calculate your moves.

POST-ENGAGEMENT ANALYSIS

Debriefing is a necessary component of every engagement.

- What went wrong?
- What went right?
- What can be improved for next time?

WRR is a training technique that describes a simple sequence which should be taken after each encounter.

W: WASH

A cleaning process the clearing evaluates the situation, determines flaws, and identifies corrections to be made

R: RINSE

Where the corrections are made and the flaws are amended, this is followed by a strategic evaluation

R: REPEAT

Now its time to the revised technique to be put into practiced and rehearsed to see if it validated

RULES OF ENGAGEMENT

What are some examples of:

Fundamentals:_____

_____

Protocols:_____

_____

Rituals:_____

_____

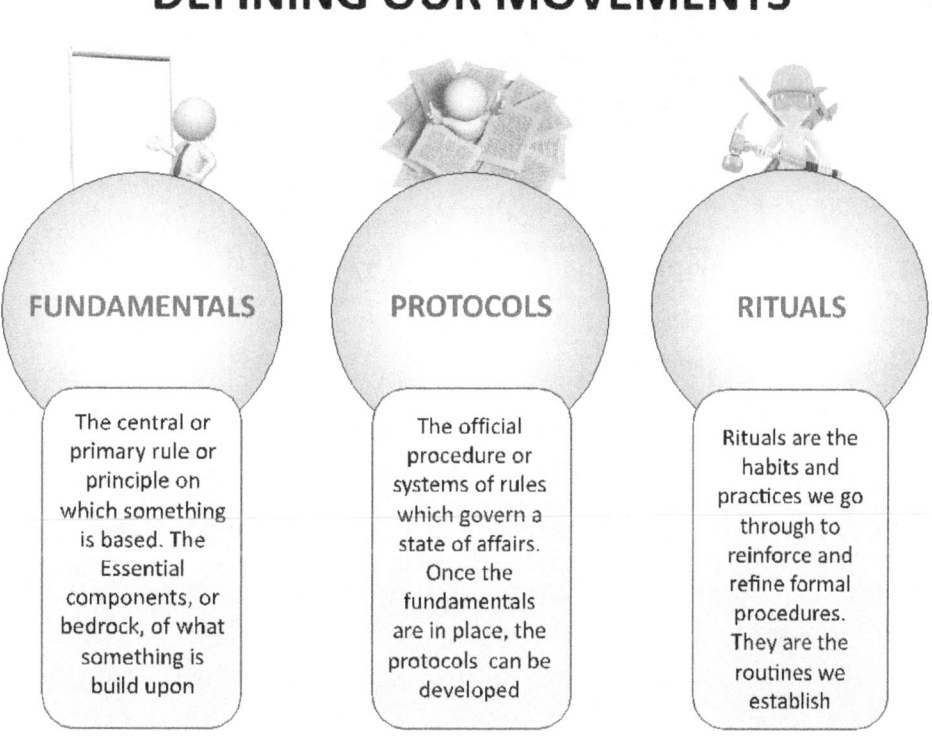

EXECUTION OF AN ENGAGEMENT

Professionalism is key in every engagement.

- **Proper**
- **Presentation**
- **Promotes**
- **Peak**
- **Performance**

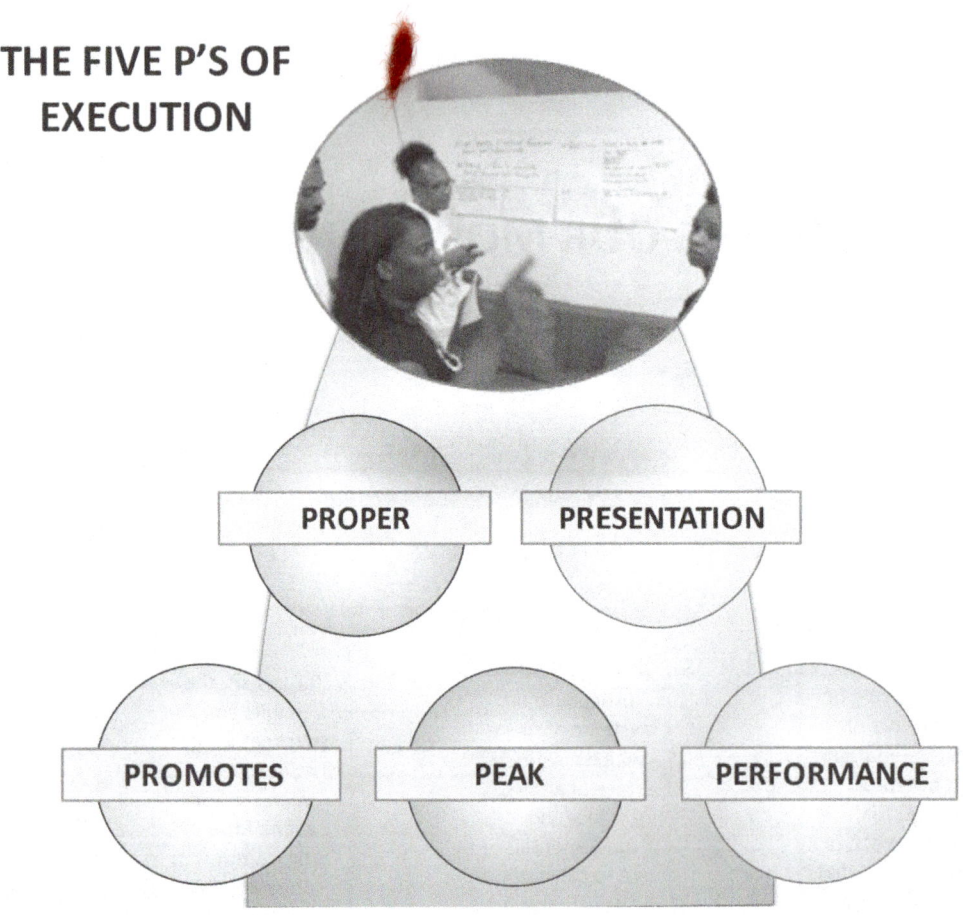

SECTION II NOTES

SECTION III

ON THE STREET SCENARIOS

Don't make excuses.

Make adjustments.

PRELIMINARY QUESTIONS FOR EVERY ENGAGEMENT

- What is the issue?

- What are the factors causing this issue?

- What are three ways this scenario could play out?

- What is the healthiest ie. violence-free response for the people involved?

- How are you going to arrive at this response?

- What are the root causes or origin of this incident?

- How could these causes be remedied to avoid future incidents?

SCENARIO QUESTIONS

- IDENTIFY THE PROBLEM(S) in this scenario. (flip chart] if available) Dialog and decide why these problems are happening.

- CURRENT FACTORS impacting the circumstances?

- THREE POTENTIAL WAYS this scenario could play out?

- HEALTHIEST RESPONSE for the people in the scenario? Why?

- IMPLEMENT THE RESPONSE, How? (E.g. referral to a conflict mediator)

- ROOT CAUSES, can you identify what might be the cause crisis or violence in this scenario? How could you address them?

SCENARIO 1

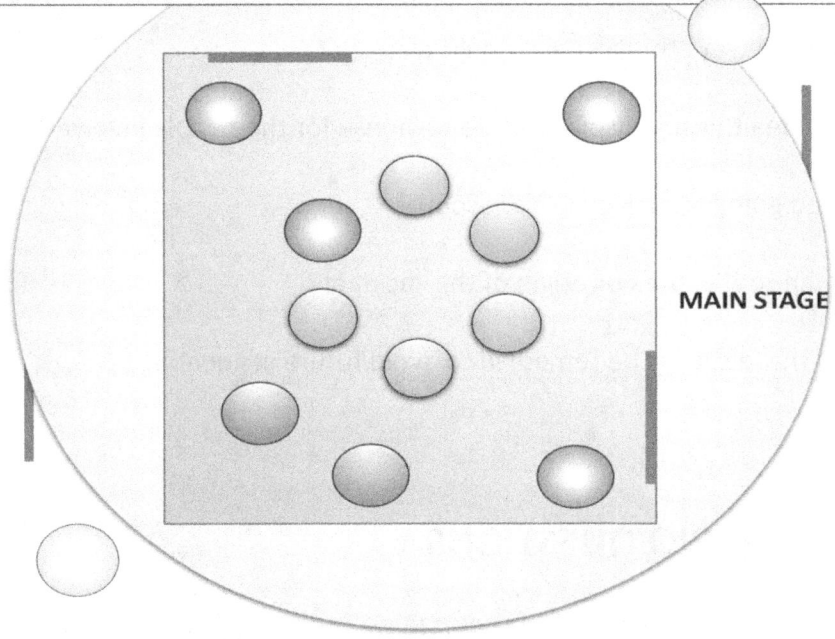

In Manual 1, you were provided this picture as an exercise, now you are tasked to explain the roles & positions of each circle, remember, the circles are controlling the room, interiorly, externally.

Two circles outside the main stage:_____

_____

Three circles in the top and bottom right corners and one in the center circle (left):_____

_____

Five center circles :_____

_____

Two circles on the bottom left:_____

_____

GO THROUGH THE SCENARIO QUESTIONS FOR SCENARIO 1:

SCENARIO 2

> Manual #1 also provided you this diagram. Your task is to analyze the picture below and solve the engagement to the best of your ability. Use the provided skill sets in this manual and manual 1

Headquarters

Sidewalk

Vernon Ave.

Determine the skills sets you will need:

1._____

2._____

3._____

What else might you need to resolve this situation? Include personal qualities.

1._____

2._____

3._____

GO THROUGH THE SCENARIO QUESTIONS FOR SCENARIO 2:

SCENARIO 3

You're Conducting A Community March Though The Neighborhood, Everything Is Going Well Until Three Cars Pull Up And Block Your Path. A Group Of Individuals Slowly Exits The Vehicles, You See They Are Have Clappers, (Guns). They Express They Have Been Told Your Team Has Been Snitching To Local Law Enforcement About Their Activities, They Want An Explanation. They Also Express They Know You're Getting Paid By The City And Ask Is That The Only Damn Reason You're In The Hood? They Express They Have Never Seen You In This Part Of Town Before! Engage

What tone of voice should you use to respond? Choose one.

  a. Respectful but firm.

  b. Apologetic.

  c. The same tone as they used to address you.

GO THROUGH THE SCENARIO QUESTIONS FOR SCENARIO 3:

SCENARIO 4

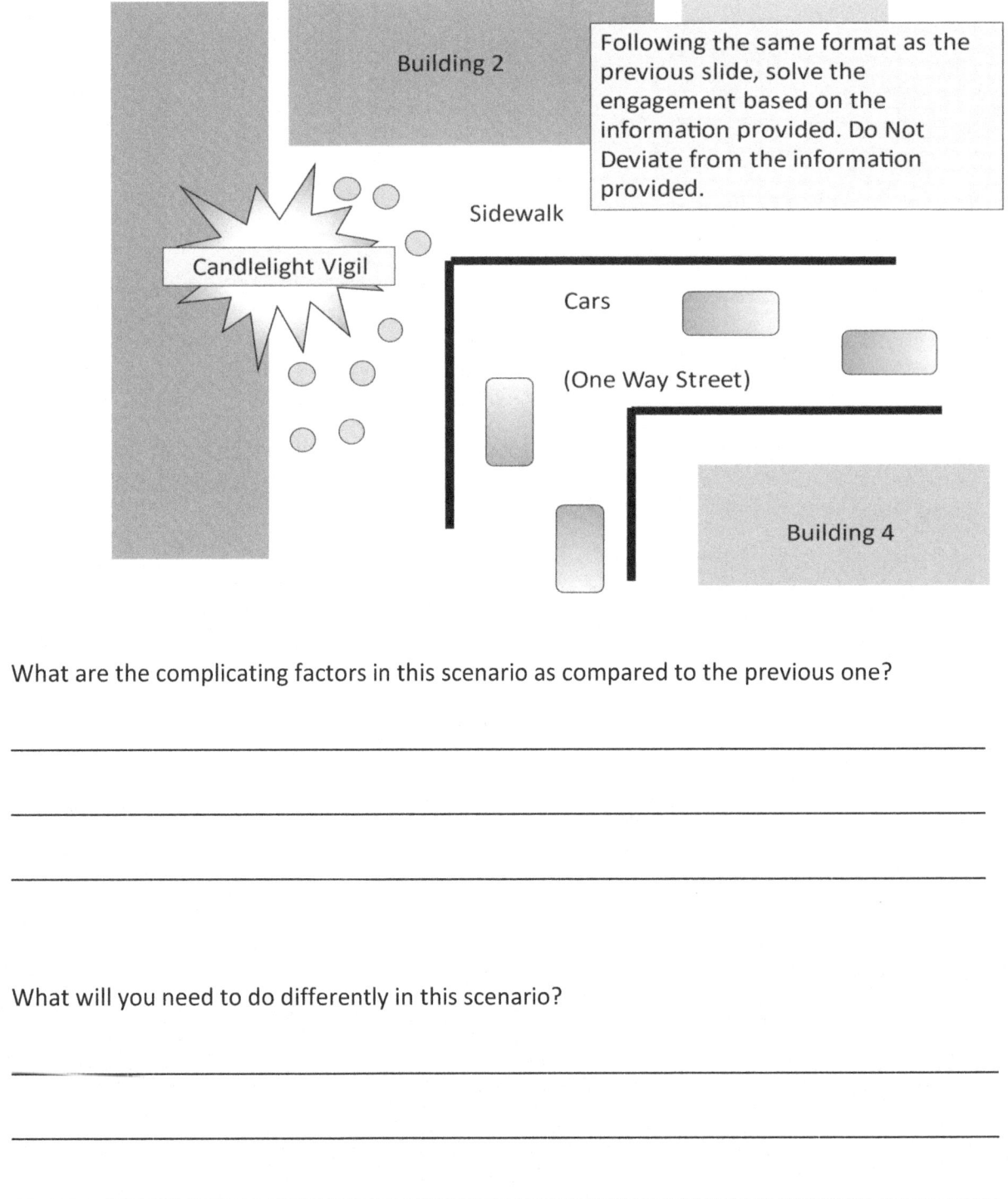

What are the complicating factors in this scenario as compared to the previous one?

_____

_____

_____

What will you need to do differently in this scenario?

_____

_____

_____

GO THROUGH THE SCENARIO QUESTIONS FOR SCENARIO 4:

SECTION III NOTES

SECTION IV

MAKING THE ENGAGEMENT SAFE AND EFFECTIVE

Misfortune usually comes in the door

that was left open for it.

STAYING COOL, CALM AND COLLECTED

Why is keeping your emotions out of the engagement of paramount importance?

_____

_____

What can you do if you feel your emotions getting the best of you?

_____

_____

THINK

This is when you have allowed your adversary to gain the upper hand because of your emotionalism as opposed to your operational discipline

- **T:** *TIME ALLOTMENT*
- **H:** *HONE-IN*
- **I:** *IDENTIFY OUTCOMES*
- **N:** *NAVIGATE CIRCUMSTANCES*
- **K:** *KICK IN WITH ACTION*

STAYING SAFE

- Think before you act.

- Be prepared, that will counteract panic.

- Take countermeasures only after analyzing their possible outcomes.

- Remain flexible.

- Look for commonalities with previous situations, but keep in mind every situation is unique.

- Know who you're dealing with. Be familiar with attack methods and predator characteristics.

- Focus on the potential victim, vulnerabilities in the physical environment.

- Determine specifics of the situation at hand.

SURVIVAL MINDSET
(RULES)

1. The psychological of urban survival is a "THINKING PERSONS PRACTICE".
2. Greatest enemy is any stress situation is panic! BEST WEAPON AGAINST PANIC IS PREPARATION.
3. Countermeasures should by taken AFTER ANALYSIS, NOT BEFORE.
4. Strategies & techniques, should remain FLEXIBLE & SITUATIONAL SPECIFIC.
5. Look for COMMON DENOMINATORS realizing every engagement is unique.
6. The focus on the adversary is limited to UNDERSTANDING PREDATORY CHARACTERISTICS & ATTACK METHODS which are relevant to the design of countermeasures.
7. PCITI's concentration is on the POTENTIAL VICTIM, HIS/HER ENVIRONMENT, AND THEIR RULES & TOOLS. Our strategy works by ANALYZING VULNERABILITIES & taking COUNTERMEASURES through which BEHAVIOR and the IMMEDIATE PHYSICAL ENVIRONMENT ARE ALTERED to reduce exposed vulnerabilities.
8. Essential to understand SPECIFIC CONDITIONS under which NEGATIVE ENGAGEMENTS TRANSPIRE so targeted strategies can be designed & put into practice.

UNDERSTANDING ANGER AND AGGRESSION

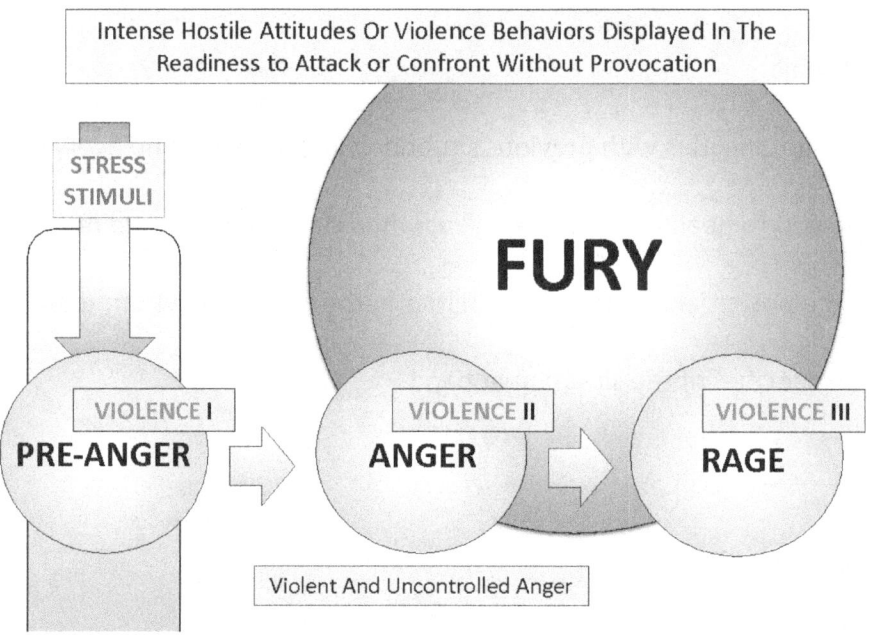

Pre-anger: Decision point, angry or not?

Anger: Strong feeling of displeasure

Rage: Violent, uncontrollable anger

Fury: Surge of extremely wild anger

Aggression: Hostile behavior, readiness to assault

- **PRE-ANGER**
  This is a place of decision, you are going to go one of two way, either anger will decide your actions are not.

- **ANGER**
  An extremely strong feeling of displeasure, annoyance, or hostility. (actually, comes from Middle English, angr=grief)

- **RAGE**
  Violent, uncontrollable anger, a vehement passion or desire coupled with a moment of aggressive behavior.

- **FURY**
  A surge of extremely wild or violence anger displaced in an individual actions and traits.

- **AGGRESSION**
  Hostile or violent behaviors, attitudes, manners towards another, readiness to confront or attack.

Give an example of:

- *Pre-anger:*_____

- *Anger:*_____

- *Rage:*_____

- *Fury:*_____

- *Aggression:*_____

THE LADDER OF VIOLENCE

Distress: Immediate emotional aftermath of a conflict.

Aggression: Hostile behavior, threats, preparing to confront.

Anger: An intensifying negative emotional response driven by feelings of being wronged or a victim of unfairness.

Violence: Acts of intentional harm to another.

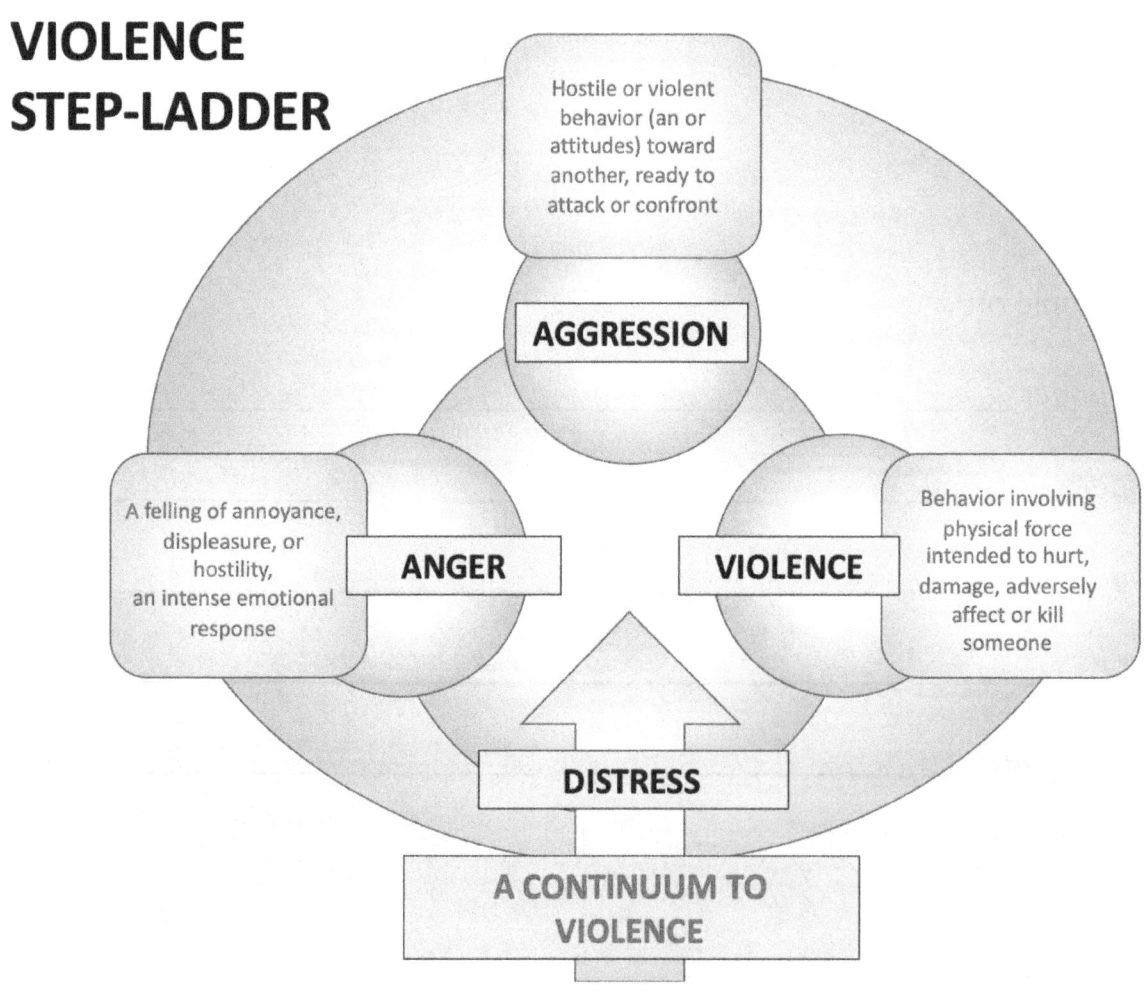

STRATEGY & PLANNING

Before engaging, formulating an action plan is crucial. Action plans should comprise:

- What is to be done.
- Who will do what.
- When steps should be taken and in what order.
- What resources and other support will be needed.
- Who should be contacted.
- What potential obstacles and resistance you may meet.

ACTION PROCESS

ACTION
"THE FACT OR PRACTICE OF DOING SOMETHING, TYPICALLY TO ACHIEVE AN AIM"

ACTIONS PLANS
Describe **How Strategies** Will Be **Implemented to Attain the Objectives.**
These Plans Refer to **Specific Action Steps** Taken to Bring About Changes Sought In All Relevant Sectors Of The Engagement.

ACTION STEPS:
Indicate What Actions Will Be Taken **(What)**
The Responsible Agents **(By Whom)**
The Timing **(When)**
Resources and Support Needed and Available, **(How)**
Potential Barriers or Resistance, And With Whom Communications About This Plan Of Action Should Occur.

SCENARIO 5

You're asked to set up A candlelight vigil for A recent 17-year-old who was shot and killed. Nobody knows why he was shot and he wasn't part of A known gang. His mother wants the vigil set up where he was killed, but there are extremely adversary forces on the ground involved in some type of battling in that area. She tells you she isn't afraid of nobody and the people who killed her son need to see a show of force, she's adamant, she wants the vigil where he was shot-case closed, engage

Apply what you have learned so far to come up with an action plan. Some things to think about:

- What is the situation?
- What is the outcome you wish to achieve?
- What tools, resources, people will you need?
- How will you keep everyone safe?

SCENARIO 5 PLAN

TEAM BUILDING

Any one interventionist is only as effective as his or her team. Building a team that operates seamlessly and smoothly is essential. When building your team,

- Set clear objectives for the purpose of your team.

- Teammates must make decisions by consensus. Egos must be put aside.

- Teammates must trust and support each other.

- Teammates must have clear lines of communication and feedback.

- Teams must have a procedure for making decisions that incorporates all members.

THE FIVE CHARACTERISTICS of T/B

- *SETTING CLEAR OBJECTIVES*

Objectives must be set in a clear manner. Goals should be specific

- *COMMITMENT OF TEAM MEMBERS*

Members work for consensus on decisions. Ideally, team members of successful groups solicit feedback on their behavior. They are also thoroughly committed to the objectives.

- *INTERACTION AMONG TEAMMATES*

Individuals trust and support their fellow teammates and involve them in decision-making.

- *LINES OF COMMUNICATION*

Team building requires a mechanism for communication between the team leader and team members and among members.

- *DEFINITIVE DECISION-MAKING PROCESS*

Follow a procedure to make decisions and solve problems. A definitive procedure removes the burden of decision making from one team member with strong opinions, allowing for all members of the group have a hand in decisions.

TEAM UNIFIED CONCEPT

- *T Together*
- *E Everyone*
- *A Achieves*
- *M More*

- *T Tactical*
- *E Evidence*
- *A Advancing*
- *M Movement*

Why is it so important to establish decision-making procedures in a team and to ensure everyone has a voice?

_____

_____

_____

_____

_____

THE PARAMETERS OF PHYSICAL SPACE

It is important to always be aware of your physical space, where you are in regard to others around you.

- *INTIMATE*: Family, loved ones, trusted friends.
- *PERSONAL*: Close friends, those with whom you feel comfortable.
- *SOCIAL*: Everyday interactions, usually with known individuals.
- *PUBLIC*: Interactions with strangers.

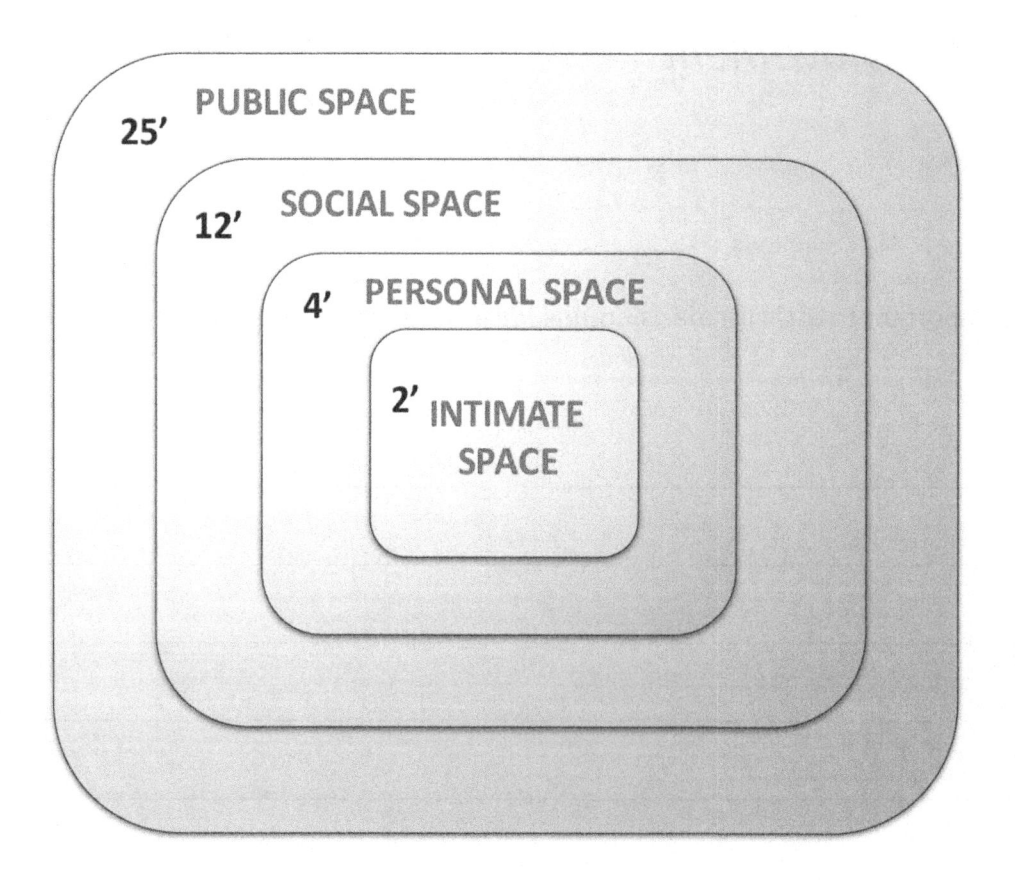

25' PUBLIC SPACE
12' SOCIAL SPACE
4' PERSONAL SPACE
2' INTIMATE SPACE

SECTION IV NOTES

SECTION V

PUTTING IT ALL TOGETHER

Your direction is more important than your speed.

EXAMINING BEHAVIOR

Interventionists must understand the role of triggers and how they play into both the internal process of thinking and the external result of behavior.

- *Perception*: Awareness of a situation.
- *Triggers*: Things, internal or external, that provoke emotional reactions.
- *Thoughts*: Mental process kicks off in response to the emotions.
- *Actions*: Behaviors that result from the mental process.
- *Consequences*: The fallout or response from the actions taken or not taken.

How does the continuum play out when triggers are removed?

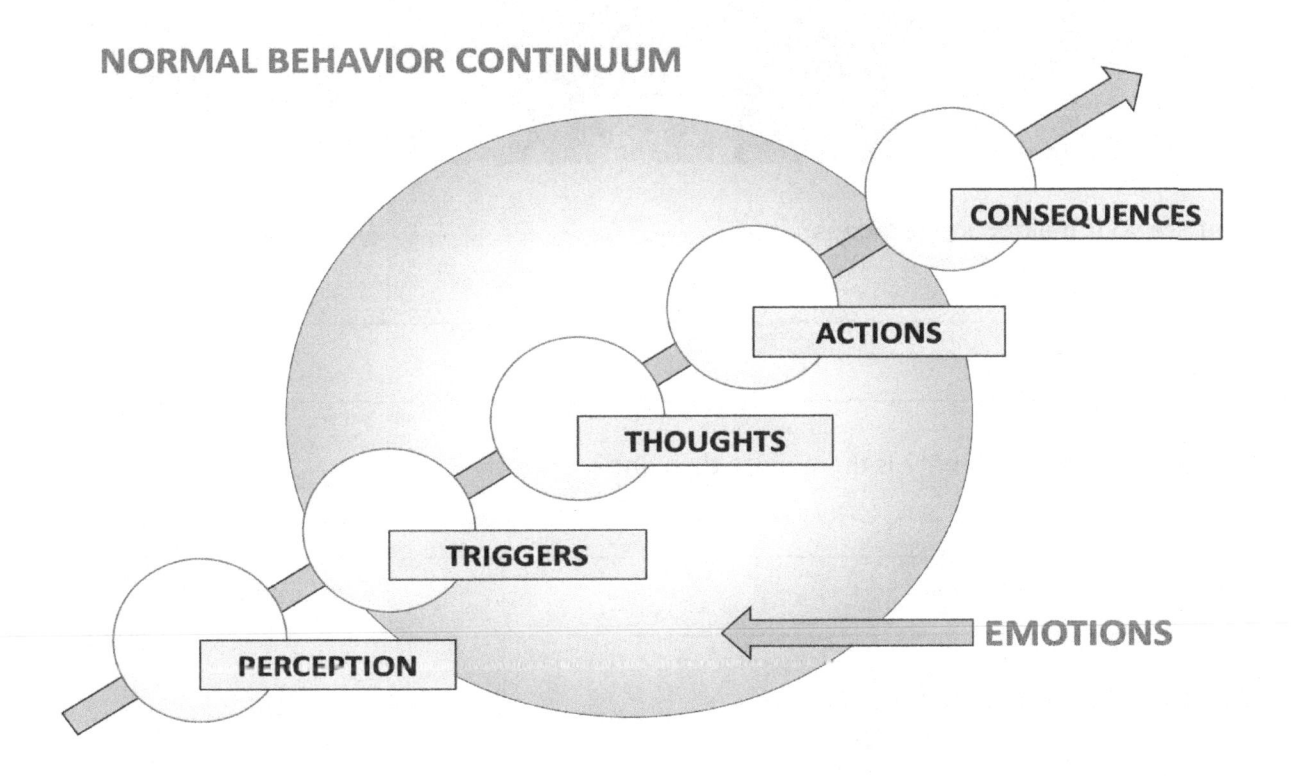

NORMAL BEHAVIOR CONTINUUM

PERCEPTION → TRIGGERS → THOUGHTS → ACTIONS → CONSEQUENCES

EMOTIONS

SCENARIO 6

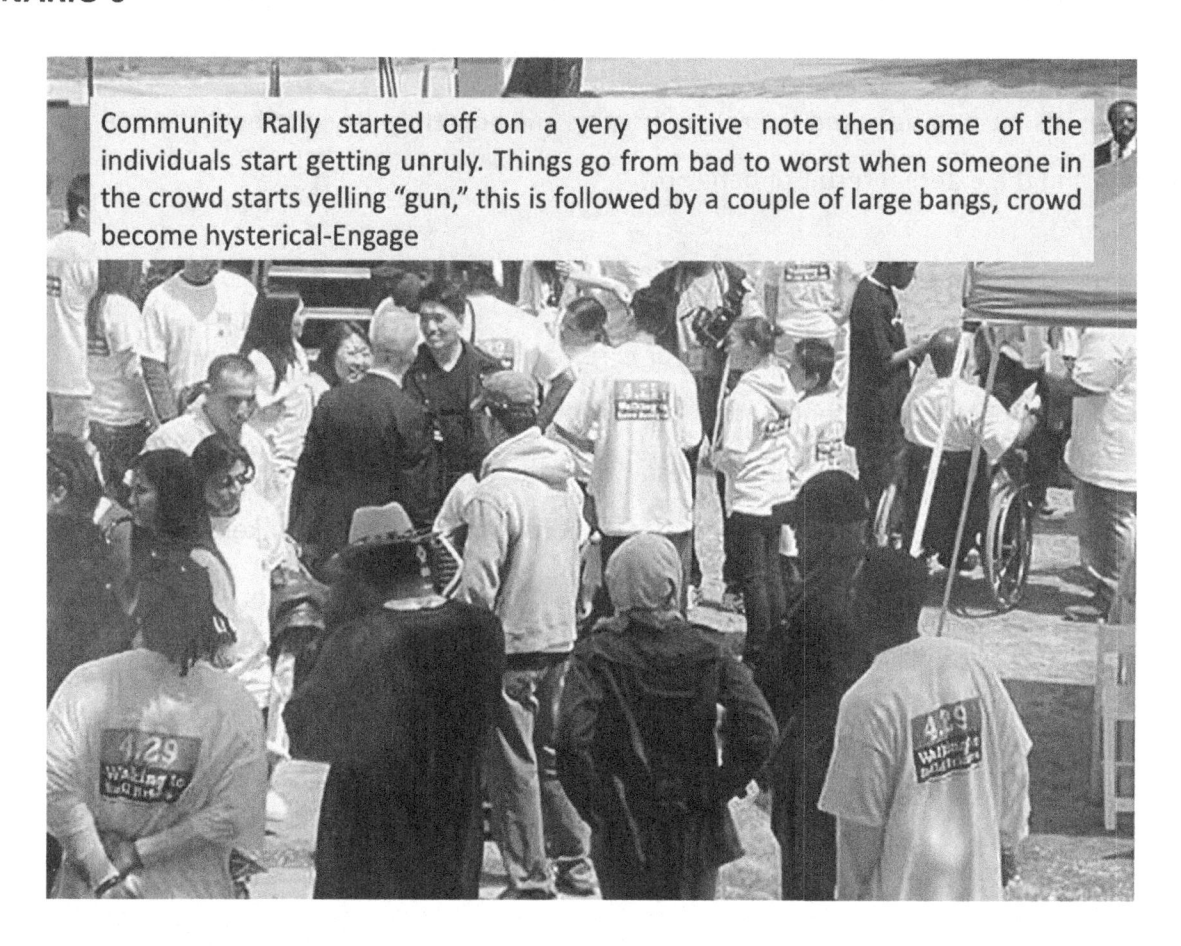

Community Rally started off on a very positive note then some of the individuals start getting unruly. Things go from bad to worst when someone in the crowd starts yelling "gun," this is followed by a couple of large bangs, crowd become hysterical-Engage

What are your major considerations?

_____

_____

What is your primary threat? Is there more than one?

_____

_____

What should your first actions be?

_____

_____

ON THE SCENE

Once you're on the scene, you must analyze the situation and determine what needs to be done in order to neutralize the threat. In some cases, you may have to use more than one of the methods delineated below to defuse the situation entirely.

- *Restore:* Get the person back to normalcy by removing what is triggering them.
- *Extract*: Identify the person who is the threat and the person who is the object of the threat. Remove the person who is the object of the threat, then work to defuse the threatening person.
- *Resolve*: Determine what is the issue of concern, provide solutions or options.
- *Repair:* Ascertain the cause of trauma, attempt to mend or heal.

METHODS OF ENGAGEMENT

- **RESTORE**
  Establish a Point of Normalcy, Get Them Back There
  Question, Remove Triggers, Replace
- **EXTRACT**
  Identify Fuse, Minimize Explosion, Secure Principle & Remove
  Identify, Remove, then Diffuse
- **RESOLVE**
  Determine Issues, Provide Answer or Suitable Option
  Pinpoint Assessment, Settle Concerns
- **REPAIR**
  Pinpoint the Trauma of Pain, Attempt to Mend
  Ascertain Need/s, Patch, Heal

SCENARIO 7

> Get The Hell Out Of My Face Fool, Aint A Dam Thing You Need To Say To Me About Nothing!

Apply Methods of Engagement to this scenario. Be specific in addressing each of the four headings.

_____

_____

_____

_____

_____

_____

WRAP UP: ANALYZING ENGAGEMENTS

Use this three-measure tool to determine how successful your actions were.

- **DATA**: Did you use information from the get-go of the incident and throughout its duration?
- **RESOURCES**: Did you utilize your interventionist toolbox throughout the engagement?
- **PROTOCOL**: Did you rely on validated procedures to achieve your results?

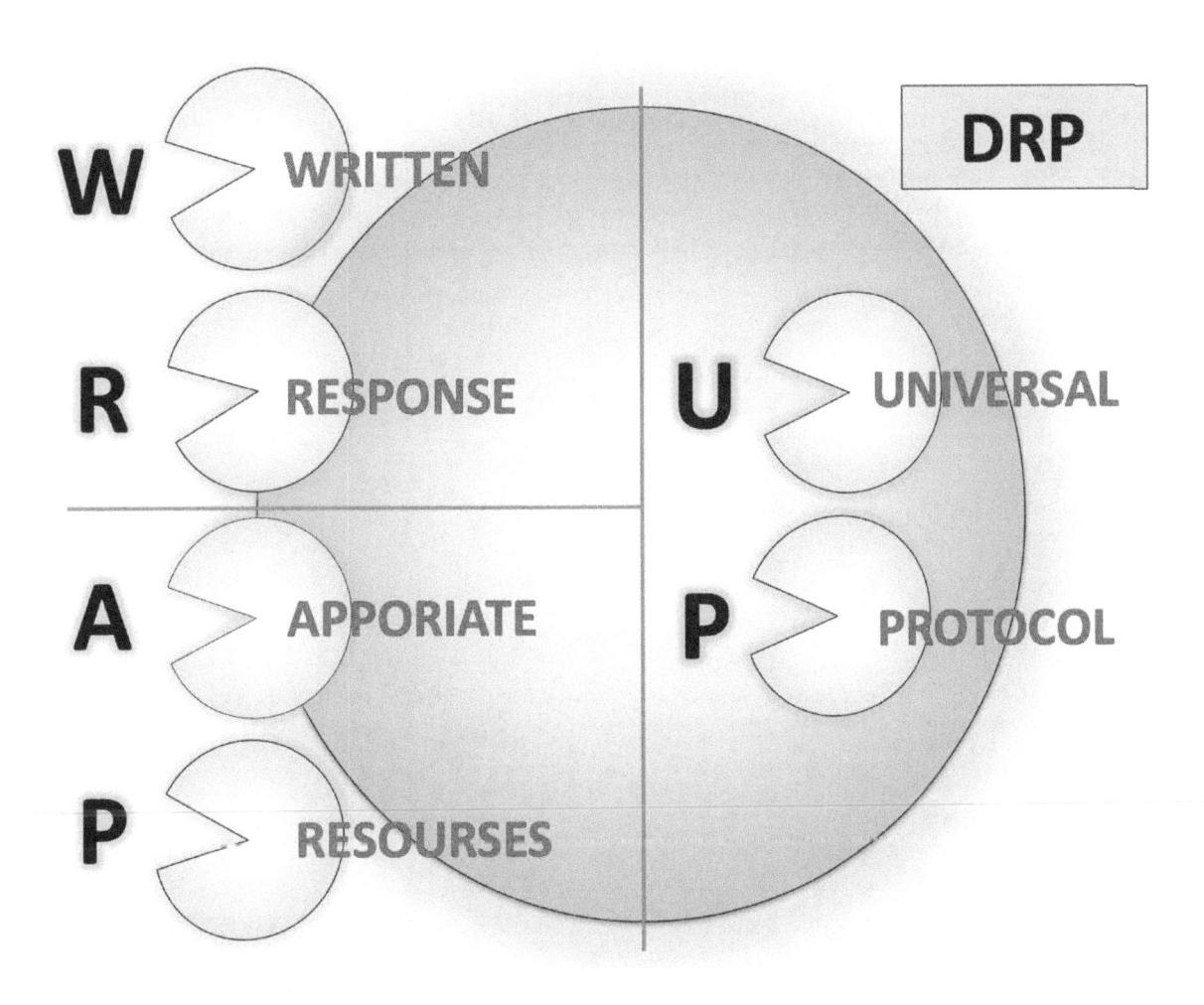

DRP

W — WRITTEN
R — RESPONSE
A — APPORIATE
P — RESOURSES

U — UNIVERSAL
P — PROTOCOL

SECTION V NOTES

TEMPLATES & TOOLS

THE PROFESSIONAL COMMUNITY INTERVENTION TRAINING INSTITUTE

501c3 NON-PROFIT BUILD PROGRAM

THE LTO MOVEMENT

1409 W. Vernon Ave. LA. CA. 90062
(800) 926-2155 Office
(213) 219-9204 Mobil
Email: takechargeinc@aol.com
Website 2: Buildprogram.org

Book:
"Peace in the Hood"
Documentaries:
"License to Operate" & "The Black Jacket"

COMMUNITY VIOLENCE INTERVENTION
TRAINING SPECIALISTS

The Build Program and its training division, the Professional Community Intervention Training Institute International, has always been at the forefront of effective leadership building, strategic planning, and the most comprehensive proactive scenario driven certification training in society today.

BUILD has become subject matter training & technical assistance experts for the White House.

- 111 U.S. Cities Trained
- 117 Municipalities
- 15 Hospitals
- 25,017 Violence Interrupters

buildprogram.org

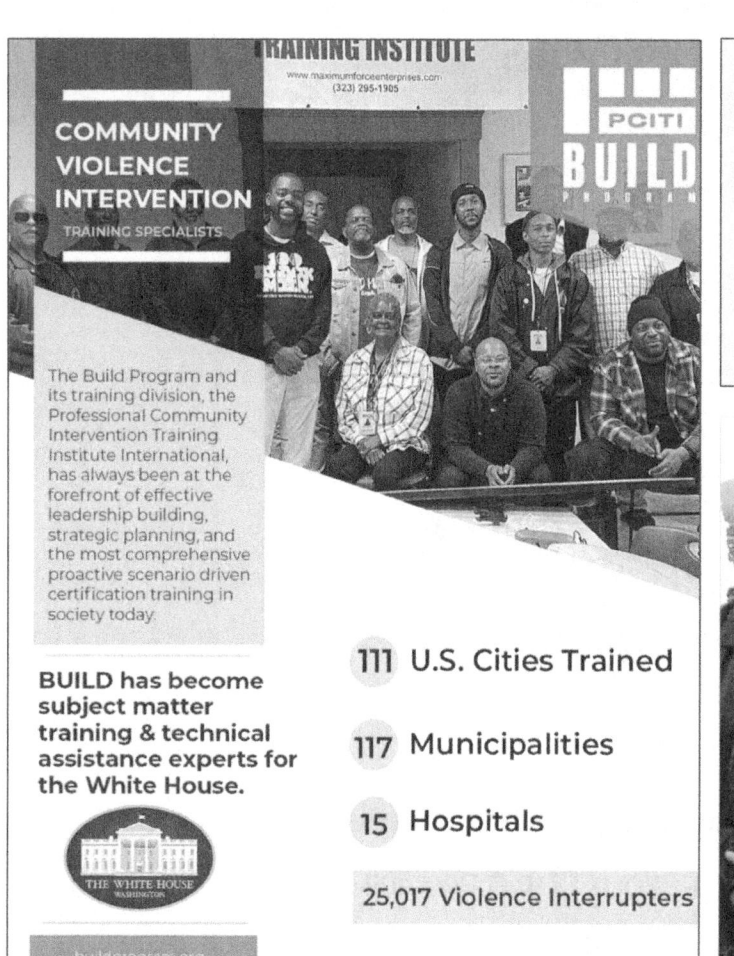

BUILD
PROFESSIONAL COMMUNITY INTERVENTION TRAINING INSTITUTE

STORIES OF SOUTH LA

PROFESSOR AQUIL BASHEER
Professional Community Interventionist & Violence Prevention Expert

Made in the USA
Las Vegas, NV
09 June 2024